Contents

D1127418

Introduction

Designed for grades 5–8, each *More Tic-Tac-Toe Math* game sheet contains nine problems in a tic-tac-toe format. Most of the game sheets focus on a common concept, such as decimals or fractions computation, metric or standard measurements, percent operations, math vocabulary, pattern perception, or area and perimeter. Throughout the game sheets, students are encouraged to use problem-solving and critical-thinking skills. They are also asked to think about the meaning of math terms as they solve problems at various levels of difficult.

How to Use

More Tic-Tac-Toe Math game masters may be used as ten-minute starter activities at the beginning of math class or as "fillers." They also may be used as short review activities, extra-credit challenges, or even as assignments for specific topics. (The Skills Planner on page vi will help you select game sheets for specific skills.) The game sheets may be used by individual students, pairs of students, or small groups.

How to Score

Students receive one point for each correct solution plus one bonus point for each "tic-tac-toe" (three correct solutions in a row, column, or diagonal). Students may earn a maximum of 17 points if all problems within a game are solved correctly. See page 99 for the Answer Key.

More Tic-Tac-Toe Math allows teachers to

- review and reinforce math concepts throughout the year
- teach problem solving every day
- provide extra-credit activities that bring more variety to each class session
- teach and reinforce math vocabulary
- present concepts in an integrated way
- provide practice in a motivating, enjoyable format
- keep concepts in all areas fresh in the minds of their students

Skills Planner

Skill	Game Number	Skill	Game Number
Algebra	65, 66	Money	21, 22, 23, 24, 25, 26, 27, 28, 35, 36, 41, 69
Analogies	67		
Angles	59, 60		
Area	61, 62, 63	Multiples	11, 76
Decimals	17, 18, 19, 20, 21, 22, 23, 24, 25, 26, 27, 28, 29, 30, 31, 33, 34, 35, 36, 76	Number Theory	11, 12, 13, 14, 15, 16
		Order of Operations	10
		Percent	35, 36
		Perimeter	61, 62, 63
Exponents	13, 14, 15, 16	Prime Numbers	71
Factors	12	Problem Solving	8, 23, 24, 25, 26, 27, 28, 35, 36, 41, 49, 57, 58, 69, 70, 73, 78, 81
Fractions	32, 37, 38, 39, 40, 41, 42, 43, 44, 45, 46, 47, 48, 49, 50, 74		
		Sequences	9, 11, 15
Geometry	59, 60, 61, 62, 63, 64	Surface Area	62, 64
Graphing	65, 66	Time	57, 58
Measurement	40, 51, 52, 53, 54, 55, 56, 57, 58, 59, 60, 61, 62, 63, 64, 70, 74, 75, 80, 81	Visualization	63, 64, 65, 66
		Vocabulary	48, 80, 82, 83, 84, 85
		Volume	62, 64
Mixed Numbers	39, 42, 48	Whole Numbers	1, 2, 3, 4, 5, 6, 7, 8, 9, 10, 68, 72, 75, 76, 77, 78, 79, 82, 83, 84

Whole Numbers

Name _____

Game 1

The numbers are 18 and 6. sum = _____ product = _____ difference = _____ quotient = _____	Fill in each box with a number from 1 through 9. ☐ X ☐ = 42	What number comes next? 1, 7, 13, 19
Complete the pattern. 6, 12, ____, ____, 30	Juan, Erika, and Bob are friends. The sum of their ages is 30. Erika is twice the age of Juan, and Bob is 5 years older than Erika. How old is Juan?	Estimate the sum. 552 ☐ 436 ☐ + 877 ☐
How many four-digit numbers can be made using the four digits, 1, 2, 3, 4, in each number?	Round to the nearest ten thousand. 5, 485, 210	Find the average of 50, 60, 70, 80, and 40.

Name _____

Game 2

2 3 □ 1 □ 9 + □ 1 4 6 1 8	What is the sum of the millions digit and the ten thousands digit? 81,234,567	3 □ 1 □ − 1 2 □ 6 1 7 5 8
How many zeros are in the number for one trillion?	0 → 1 1 → 3 2 → 5 3 → 7 If this pattern continues then 59 → □	How many months have exactly 30 days? List those months.
5 6 x 3 □ 1 1 2 1 □ 8 □ □ 9 2	Write in words: 6,005,004,001	2 0 1 □ ⟌ 1 2 □ 6

Name _____

Game 3

3 1 2 9 + ☐ ☐ ☐ —————— 4 0 2 8	5,985,764 What is the product of the hundred thousands digit and the hundreds digit?	5 1 2 3 – ☐ ☐ ☐ —————— 4 4 4 5
Write this number in words 100,001,025	0 → 1 1 → 3 5 → 11 3 → 7 6 → ☐ What rule explains this?	How many years are in a century?
8 5 3 13)☐☐☐☐☐	Round to the nearest thousand. 8,181,818	6 0 8 x 7 6 —————— ☐☐☐☐ ☐☐☐☐ ☐☐☐☐☐

Name _____

Game 4

The 6 in 324,657 stands for _____ .	Complete the pattern. 9, 3, 18, 6, ____ , 12	300,000 + 60,000 + 500 + 40 =
$6 \times (5 + 8) =$ $(5 + 8) \times$ ☐	$1 + 3 = 4$ $1 + 3 + 5 = 9$ $1 + 3 + 5 + 7 = 16$ If the pattern continues, what numbers will give a sum of 100?	If $A = 15$ $B = 6$ $C = 8,$ then $A + C - B =$ ☐
Which is another way to express $6 \times 6 \times 6$? a. $6 + 3$ b. 3×6 c. 3^6 d. 6^3	I ordered 50 cartons of straws. Each carton contained 100 straws. How many straws came in my order?	A box contains 367 marbles. 189 are red. How many are not red?

Name _____

Game 5

Circle the billions digit. 1 2 3,4 5 6,7 8 9,1 0 2	Fill in each box with a number from 0 through 9. □ x □ = 48	What number comes next? 1, 8, 4, 32, 16,
Complete the pattern. 7, 14, 21, ___, ___, 42	I am thinking of two numbers. Their sum is 100. Their product is 1600. Their quotient is four. What is the difference of the two numbers?	Estimate the product. 6 8 4 □ x 5 6 □
Is zero an even number?	Round to the nearest hundred thousand. 8,659,483	7⟌4 0 9 5

Name _____

Game 6

Fill in each box with +, −, x, ÷. 8 ☐ 9 = 72 8 ☐ 9 = 17	Unscramble this math word: D O T A N I D I	18 → 54 5 → 15 30 → 90 **What rule explains this?**
The number of stripes on the U.S. flag + The number of stars on the U.S. flag = .	If you write the whole numbers from 1 through 60, how many times will you write the digit 4?	6 x 8 = ☐ 48 ÷ 6 = ☐ 48 ÷ 8 = ☐
I am a number between 8 x 9 and 6 x 14. I am a multiple of 3 but not 5. I am odd. What number am I?	3 is to 4 as 24 is to _____. The answer is *not* 25.	How much more is 18 + 16 x 5 than 56 − 12 ÷ 4?

Game 7

Circle the hundred thousands digit. 1,234,567	1 → 2 2 → 4 3 → 8 If this pattern continues, then 10 → ☐	Find the average of 6, 12, 18, 24, and 30.
What is the quotient of (76 + 24) divided by (36 – 11)?	1 → 1 1 + 2 → 3 1 + 2 + 3 → 6 If this pattern continues, what numbers will give a sum of 55?	If A = 19 B = 9 C = 5, then A + C x B = ☐
$2^3 \times 3^2 =$	An unsharpened pencil is approximately how long? a. 4 meters b. 8 inches c. 1 millimeter d. 10 centimeters	If three cats eat a total of six mice every day, how many mice will the cats eat in one year (not a leap year)?

Name _____

Game 8

The sum of 8 x 7 and 9 x 6 is _____.	How are the numbers 13 and 17 alike? Name three ways.	The product of 7 x 7 and 8 x 8 is _____.
If four boys share equally two candy bars, how much will each boy get?	 Which number in each triangle can you trade so that both triangles have the same sum?	If two girls share equally four candy bars, how much will each get?
Which is the correct way to solve the above problem about candy bars? a. 4 ÷ 2 b. 2 ÷ 4 c. 4 x 2	How is 4 ÷ 2 different from 2 ÷ 4?	Which is the correct way to solve the above problem about candy bars? a. 4 ÷ 2 b. 2 ÷ 4 c. 2 x 4

Game 9

$1 \times 1 =$ _____

$2 \times 2 =$ _____

$3 \times 3 =$ _____

$4 \times 4 =$ _____

These answers are called _____ numbers.

$1 \times 2 =$ _____

$1 \times 2 \times 3 =$ _____

$1 \times 2 \times 3 \times 4 =$ _____

$1 \times 2 \times 3 \times 4 \times 5 =$ _____

$1 \times 2 \times 3 \times 4 \times 5 \times 6 =$ _____

What is the sum of the tenth odd number and the tenth even number?

Unscramble this math word:

V O D I N I S I

I have $2.25 in nickels and quarters. I have three more nickels than quarters.

I have _____ nickels

and _____ quarters.

I am thinking of a number. It has two digits. When I reverse the digits and then add the new number, to the original number, I get 33. What is the number?

$1^2 =$ _____

$2^2 =$ _____

$3^2 =$ _____

$4^2 =$ _____

$5^2 =$ _____

What numbers do these Roman numerals stand for?

V = _____

IX = _____

XXIV = _____

L = _____

M = _____

Complete the pattern.

1, 4, _____, _____, 25, 36, 49, _____, _____, 100

Game 10

Add Parentheses to make this true. $3 \times 8 + 6 \div 2 = 21$	Complete the phrase. four w _____ in one m _____	$18 \div 2 + 7 \times 10 =$ a. 160 b. 79 c. none of the above
Is the statement true or false? 64 ounces > 5 pounds	Add, subtract, multiply, or divide. Use each number exactly once to get an answer of 11. 9 8 3	Write the sum of the first ten whole numbers.
$16 + 8 \div 2 - 10 \times 2 =$	Unscramble this math word: THEMAMITACS	Add parentheses to make this true. $10 \times 3 + 2 - 8 = 42$

Number Theory

Game 11

List all the factors of 80.	List the first five multiples of 40.	List all the factors of 48.
List the first five multiples of 80.	I am thinking of a number between 1 and 100. It is a palindrome and also a multiple of 5. What is the number?	What is the least common multiple of 40 and 60?
List the first 5 multiples of 60.	What is the least common multiple of 60 and 80?	3.5, 7, 10.5, 14 If this pattern continues what will be the tenth number?

Game 12

Write the prime factorization of 12. (Use exponents.)	Which number is a multiple of 16? a. 4 b. 20 c. 8 d. 32 e. 86	Write the prime factorization of 24. (Use exponents.)
Which number is a palindrome? a. 231 b. 323 c. 56 d. 102	$A + B + C + D = 35$ $A + B = 22$ $C + D = 13$ $A = B + 2$ $C = \frac{1}{2}$ of A $D =$	Which number is a factor of 16? a. 48 b. 72 c. 100 d. 8 e. 6
What is the sum of the square roots of 225 and 196?	Which number is divisible by 4 with no remainder? a. 43,881 b. 15,830 c. 32,120 d. 62,262	Which number is prime? a. 37,125 b. 1,212 c. 806 d. 97 e. 72

Game 13

$2^3 + 3^2 =$	$32 - 3^2 =$	Why is 9 called a *square number?*
5^3 means $\boxed{} \times \boxed{} \times \boxed{}$.	I earn 1¢ on January 1. I earn 3¢ on January 2. I earn 6¢ on January 3. I earn 10¢ on January 4. If this pattern continues, on what date will I earn 55¢?	$81 = 9^{\boxed{}}$
$16 = \boxed{}^4$	$10^2 - 4^3 =$	if $2^3 = 8$ $2^2 = 4$ $2^1 = 2,$ then what does 2^0 equal?

© Dale Seymour Publications®

More Tic-Tac-Toe Math

Game 14

Circle the number written in standard form. 5^2 4280 3.5×10^4	$10^3 =$	Write in standard form. 3×10^3
$3.1 \times 10^3 =$	Mary is twice as old as Feodor. In 8 years their ages will total 70. How old is each now?	$10^4 =$
Write in scientific notation. 7342	$100,000 = 10^\square$	When scientists write 4280 as 4.28×10^3, they are using _____ _____ .

Game 15

What is the sum of the first 10 square numbers?	What number comes next? 1, 4, 9, 16, 25,	Why is 225 a square number?
How many square numbers are there between 0 and 1000?	I am a number. If you take away $\frac{1}{3}$ of me, then take away $\frac{1}{3}$ of the remaining part of me, and finally take away $\frac{1}{3}$ of what is left, there will be 8 left over. What number am I?	How many triangular numbers are there between 0 and 100?
What is the sum of the first five triangular numbers?	What number comes next? 1, 3, 6, 10, 15	Why is 15 a triangular number?

Game 16

The sum of two numbers is 15. The product of the same numbers is 56. What are the two numbers?	$\square^2 + \square^2 = 25$	The difference of two numbers is 1. The product of the same two numbers is 42. What are the two numbers?
$\square^2 + \square^2 = 61$	$2^4 = 16$ $2^3 = 8$ $2^2 = 4$ $2^1 = 2$ $2^0 = $	$2^3 + \square = 23$
I am thinking of two numbers. Their product is 18. If you write the two numbers as a fraction, the fraction in lowest terms is $\frac{1}{2}$. What are the numbers?	$\square^2 + 18 = 9 \times 6$	The sum of three numbers is 60. The greatest number is two more than the least number. What are the three numbers?

Decimals and Percent

Name _____

Game 17

Underline the tens digit place, and circle the tenths digit. 1 2 3 4.5 6 7 8	Do not use a calculator. 3.2 – 1.07 =	Write this number in words. 103.001
Circle the greatest number. 0.500 0.50 0.51 0.05	Jamal made 100 pizzas in 5 days. Each day he made 5 more than he had on the previous day. How many pizzas had he made at the end of the fourth day?	What number comes next? 0.7, 0.8, 0.9
Write the number for one thousand one and five hundredths in standard form.	Do not use a calculator. 3.16 x 0.8	Arrange in order from least to greatest. 1.5 0.15 1.05

Game 18

Underline the hundreds digit, and circle the hundredths digit. 9 8 7 6.5 4 3 2	Do not use a calculator. Place the decimal point correctly in the answer. 8.99 x 0.8765 = 7 8 7 9 7 3 5	Write this number in words. 3015.05
Round to the nearest tenth. 305.453	Sue shot 100 baskets in 5 days. Each day she shot 7 more than she had on the previous day. How many baskets did she shoot on the first day?	What number comes next? 0.97, 0.98, 0.99
Write the number for two thousand two and two thousandths in standard form.	Do not use a calculator. 0. 0 0 3 8 x 4. 6 ☐☐☐☐☐ ☐☐☐☐☐ ☐☐☐☐☐☐	Arrange in order from greatest to least. 3.014 3.14 30.4 3.2

Game 19

Underline the thousands digit, and circle the thousandths digit. 1 2 3 4.5 6 7 8	0.5 + 0.3 x 0.2 =	Write this number in words. 2015.0025
Round to the nearest hundredth. 5683.998	Chizu watched 120 minutes of TV in 5 days. Each day she watched 10 more minutes than she had the previous day. How much TV did she watch on the fourth day?	What number comes next? 0.997, 0.998, 0.999
Write the number for five hundred five and five hundred ten-thousandths in standard form.	Place the decimal point correctly in the answer. Do not use a calculator. 0.156 x 0.39 —————— 006084	Arrange in order from least to greatest. 2.015 2.5 0.25 2.06

Name _____

Game 20

What is wrong with this problem? $0.2 \times 0.3 = 0.6$	Complete the phrase. four q _____ in one g _____	What is wrong here? 26.2 − 5.24 ———— 21.04
$4 \times 4 \times 4 =$ $3 \times 3 \times 3 =$ $2 \times 2 \times 2 =$ $1 \times 1 \times 1 =$ These answers are called cubic numbers.	A baseball team played 20 games, winning 8 more games than it lost. How many games did it win? How many did it loose?	Continue the pattern. $64 \rightarrow 32$ $32 \rightarrow 16$ $16 \rightarrow 8$ ☐ → ☐ ☐ → ☐ ☐ → ☐
Which pair has the sum of 1.0? a. $0.3 + 7$ b. $0.6 + 0.04$ c. $0.2 + 0.8$ d. None of the above	Unscramble this math word. ROFTAC	Does $0.4 = 0.400$?

Game 21

What number is one hundredth less than 1.0?	What is the value of 4 pennies, three nickels, and seven quarters? Express as a decimal.	What number is nine tenths more than 0.85?
$\begin{array}{r}\boxed{}\\-\ 3.7\\\hline 4.5\end{array}$	The sum of three numbers is 6. The smallest number is 0.5 times the middle number. The largest number is 1.5 times the middle number. What is the middle number?	$\begin{array}{r}\boxed{}\\+\ 2.96\\\hline 14.80\end{array}$
Continue the pattern. 0, 0.7, 1.4, 2.1 _____, _____	What is four cents less than one dime? Express as a decimal.	I buy two loaves of bread at $1.55 each, one gallon of milk at $2.98, and three pounds of apples at $.51 per pound. What is my change from a $10 bill?

Name _____

Game 22

What number is one tenth less than one?	What decimal represents the value of nine pennies, nine dimes, and nine quarters? Express as a decimal.	What number is eight hundredths more than 1.5?
Do not use a calculator. ☐☐☐☐☐ $0.05\overline{)2\ 0\ 5}$	☐　⊞　⊞⊞ 　1　　2　　3 If this pattern continues, how many small squares will be in the ninth drawing?	$\square\overline{)20.8}$ 2.6
Continue the pattern. 0.8, 1.6, 2.4, 3.2, _____, _____	What is eight dimes less than six quarters? Express as a decimal.	I bought seven granola bars at two for $1.44 and five pounds of apples at $.48 a pound. What was my change from a $20 bill?

More Tic-Tac-Toe Math

Game 23

I bought 10 pounds of onions at $0.39 per pound. I also bought 5 grapefruit at $0.49 each. What was my change if I gave the cashier a $10 bill?	I added some prices on my calculator, and the display showed 1.6. How much money is that?	I buy ten gallons of gas at $1.65 per gallon and two quarts of oil at $1.55 per quart. How much change do I get back from a $20 bill?
If I take piano lessons and my teacher charges $25.00 per lesson, how many lessons can I take for $1125?	My dad is 20 years older than I. How old was my dad when my age was exactly $\frac{1}{3}$ of his age?	An apple costs twice as much as a banana. If apples sell three for $0.96, how much will eight apples and ten bananas cost?
Is the statement true or false? Each piece of fruit costs the same when 6 apples sell for $0.96 and 8 oranges sell for $1.28.	I worked 45 hours at $6.65 per hour. You worked 37 hours at $7.35 per hour. How much more did I earn than you?	Unscramble this math word. TROALUCALC

Game 24

My family stopped for breakfast at Fast Food Delight. Each of the four of us ordered an Egg Sandwich at $1.52 each. What was our change from a $10 bill?	Turkey Tidbits cost 6 for $1.82, 9 for $2.49, or 20 for $4.65. Which is the cheapest price per tidbit?	Fast-Food Delight is open from 6:00 A.M. to 10:30 P.M. on weekdays, 6:00 A.M. to 11:00 P.M. on Saturdays, and 7:00 A.M. to 11:00 A.M. on Sundays. How many hours per week is Fast-Food Delight open?
Which is a better buy? 8-ounce cola for $0.90 or 12-ounce cola for $1.20	Jumbo burger: $1.95 Cheeseburger: $0.69 Medium Fries: $0.99 Small cola: $0.90 I spent $5.79. What did I buy?	I bought Turkey Tidbits at 20 for $4.65. If I paid $27.90, how many tidbits did I buy?
The starting wage at Fast-Food Delight was $4.75 per hour. At that wage, how many hours did I need to work in order to earn $300? (Taxes were not deducted from my pay.)	At the above prices, how many cheeseburgers can be bought with a $20 bill?	If 15¢ per dollar is deducted from my pay for taxes, how much would my pay be for 40 hours at the starting wage of $4.75 per hour?

Game 25

A calculator display shows 0.3. How much money does that represent?	Round to the nearest cent. $1.8973	I have 35¢. If that amount doubles tomorrow and then that amount doubles the next day, and if this pattern continues, how much money will I have after one week?
The price of my meal at a restaurant was $32.50. I left a 15% tip for the waiter. How much was the tip?	How many ways are there to make change for a quarter, using only pennies, nickels, and dimes?	A birthday gift for a teacher costs $20.70. If five people share the cost equally, how much does each pay?
What is the fewest coins (pennies, nickels, dimes, and quarters) that will add up to 89¢?	Write the decimal number for 7 cents.	If mints sell three for 25¢, how many can I buy with a $20 bill?

Name _____

Game 26

I buy a used car for $6000. If this cost is divided equally over 5 years, how much will I pay each month?	If you are paid 10¢ per inch, how much will you earn for one yard?	How much can I save if I buy 12 loaves of bread at three loaves for $3.85 rather than at $1.55 each?
Hamburger: $1.28 French fries: $1.16 Milk shakes: $1.55 How much do three hamburgers, a milkshake, and two orders of fries cost?	How many ways are there to make change for a half-dollar, using pennies, nickels, dimes, and quarters?	$5.02 − 3.97 ‾‾‾‾
A professional basketball player earned $3,000,000 one year. A teacher earned $30,000 that same year. How many teachers could be hired with a basketball player's salary?	If you were paid $0.01 the first second, $0.02 the next second, $0.03 the third second, and if this pattern continued, how much would you earn in 1 minute?	I bought a stereo. I made a down payment of $49.50 and then paid $29.50 per month for 2 years. How much did I pay for the stereo?

© Dale Seymour Publications®

More Tic-Tac-Toe Math

Game 27

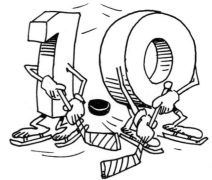

Write the decimal number for 3 pennies.	In Oregon, stores will pay a refund of 5¢ for a soda can. While there on vacation, I returned in some soda cans and received $7.15. How many cans did I return?	I bought some groceries at the store. I gave the clerk $20.00 and received $8.57 back. How much did I spend?
I earn $6.35 per hour. I work 40 hours. How much do I earn?	Some passengers get on a bus. At the first stop, eight get off and four get on. At the second stop, six get off and three get on. At the last stop, all 23 passengers get off. How many started out the trip?	How many quarters can I get in exchange for 40 nickels?
What is the greatest amount of money I can have if I have five American coins, including three different kinds of coin each worth less than 50¢?	Which is the largest amount of money? 9 quarters 23 dimes 50 nickels $3.75	I have twice as many quarters as dimes, twice as many dimes as nickels, and twice as many nickels as pennies. If I have only 1 penny, how much money do I have?

More Tic-Tac-Toe Math

Game 28

Write this number in words: 5002.064	Round the answer to the nearest dollar. $5.49 + $9.50 + $12.48 =	Put the correct sign (<, >, or =) between the numbers. 5.09 ☐ 5.104
3 + 1.34 =	Pencils: 3 for 25¢ Erasers: 3 for 49¢ Notebook 76¢ per paper: package What is the cost of 3 packages of notebook paper and 5 pencils?	If I buy groceries that cost $0.69, $1.57, and $2.69, about how much do I spend? Estimate your answer.
1 5 .4 x 0 .4 5 ☐☐☐ ☐☐☐ ☐☐☐☐☐	Write 12.34 in expanded form.	10 ÷ 0.5 =

Game 29

Write this number in words. 0.0469	Round to the nearest cent. $567.124	Write the number for five and six thousandths in standard form.
0.375 + 0.39 + 3.04 =	Week 1 → 0.5 Week 2 → 1.0 Week 3 → 2.0 Week 4 → 4.0 Week 5 → 8.0 If this pattern continues, then Week 10 → ☐	If I spend $13.98, $4.79, and $2.29, about how much do I spend. Estimate your answer.
Write 7413 in expanded form.	0 . 0 0 4 5 x 3 .2 ☐☐☐☐☐ ☐☐☐☐☐ ☐☐☐☐☐☐	67 − 38.6

Game 30

0.3 x 0.4 =	0.3 + 0.4 =	6.3 – 3.85 =
$(0.03)^2 =$	If $A = 100$ $B = 10$ $C = 1$ and if the pattern continues, what is F worth?	$(1.25)^2 =$
If 5 pounds of potatoes cost $2.19, how much will 30 pounds cost?	Write in lowest terms the fraction that equals 0.05.	If I work 8 hours and 15 minutes and if I earn $5.60 per hour, how much will my pay be?

Game 31

Add three tenths, four hundredths, and two thousands.	$0.6 +$ ☐ $= 2.1$	Add two thousandths, five tens, and three tenths.
Round to the nearest thousandth. 84.5368	Which is greater? 27 hundredths or 37 thousandths	$0.08 +$ ☐ $= 1.2$
Subtract two and one tenth from three and five hundredths.	Round to the nearest one. 5.9004	Write the decimal number that is exactly halfway between 0.01 and 0.02.

Game 32

$$5 + \boxed{} = 9$$

$$\frac{5}{12} + \frac{\boxed{}}{\boxed{}} = \frac{3}{4}$$

$$0.5 + \boxed{} = 0.9$$

$$\frac{\boxed{}}{6} + \frac{\boxed{}}{6} = \frac{1}{3}$$

Write the answer in lowest terms.

$$\boxed{} \quad \frac{5}{12} \text{ cm}$$

$$\frac{3}{4} \text{ cm}$$

perimeter =

$$\frac{5}{12} - \frac{\boxed{}}{12} = \frac{1}{4}$$

$$0.9 - 0.5 =$$

Write the answer in lowest terms.

$$\frac{3}{4} - \frac{5}{12} =$$

$$9 - 5 =$$

Game 33

Write $\frac{1}{2}$ as a decimal.	What is the sum of the tens digit and the hundredths digit? 123.456	What is the sum of the thousandths digit and the ones digit? 143.852
Round to the nearest hundredth. 25.7345	Write the decimal number that is exactly halfway between 1.6 and 1.7.	Write $\frac{1}{4}$ as a decimal.
Write the number for two and three thousandths in standard form.	Circle the ten thousandths digit. 123.45678	Write the number for sixty-three and fifty-one hundredths in standard form.

Game 34

Add five tenths and three hundredths.	Does 1.5 equal 1.50?	$\begin{array}{r} 4.3 \\ -\,0.012 \\ \hline \end{array}$
Multiply three tenths and two tenths.	Write the decimal number that is exactly halfway between 0.5 and 0.6.	$0.5 + 0.03 =$
Subtract twelve thousandths from four and three tenths.	Which is greater? two tenths or nine thousandths	$0.3 \times 0.2 =$

Name _____

Game 35

The percent sign (%) means _____ 3% means 3 x [　　　]	Complete the phrase. 28 d _____ in F _____	$5\frac{1}{4}$% equals what decimal number?
Is the statement true or false? 300% = 3	I went shopping. In the first store I spent $12.50. In the next store I spent $8.75. In the last store I spent $10.25. If I have $25 left, how much money did I start with?	Complete the pattern. 5%　$\frac{5}{100}$　0.05 —　$\frac{10}{100}$　0.10 15%　—　0.15 20%　$\frac{20}{100}$　0.20
I deposit $500 in a bank savings account. If my money earns 3% every year, how much interest will I have earned at the end of one year?	I purchased $96.50 worth of items from a store. If there is a 5% sales tax, how much will my total bill be?	In a recent math test, my score was 80%. If there were 50 questions, how many did I get correct?

© Dale Seymour Publications®

Game 36

Which statement is false? a. 5% of 90 = 4.5 b. 20% of 50 = 10 c. 80% of 40 = 30 d. 40% of 500 = 200	Six is what percent of 30?	A math test had 50 questions, and I missed 6. What percent did I get?
49% of 80 is about how much? Estimate your answer.	50% of a number is 2 less than 25% of 28. What is the number?	A bicycle that regularly costs $245.00 is on sale at 20% off the regular price. What is the sale price?
My bill at a cafe was $15.00, and I added a 15% tip. How much change should I have gotten from a $20 bill?	A book is priced at $12. The sales tax is 6%. What is the total cost of the book?	Which statement is true? a. 6 is 50% of ten. b. 5 is 10% of 50. c. 10 is 25% of 30. d. 75 is 60% of 200.

Fractions and Mixed Numbers

Game 37

Shade in $\frac{1}{2}$ of the circles. ○ ○ ○ ○ ○ ○ ○ ○ ○ ○ ○ ○	Shade in $\frac{1}{3}$ of the circles. ○ ○ ○ ○ ○ ○ ○ ○ ○ ○ ○ ○	Which is greater? $\frac{1}{2}$ or $\frac{1}{3}$
Add a half dozen and a third of a dozen.	$\frac{1}{2} - \frac{1}{3} =$	Write the answer in lowest terms. $\frac{6}{12} =$
$\frac{1}{2}$ of 12 =	$\frac{1}{3}$ of 12 =	Write the answer in lowest terms. $\frac{4}{12} =$

Game 38

Shade in $\frac{3}{4}$ of the

Shade in $\frac{2}{3}$ of the squares.

Shade in $\frac{3}{4}$ of the circles.

Shade in $\frac{2}{3}$ of the squares.

Add $\frac{3}{4}$ of 12 and $\frac{2}{3}$ of 9.

Shade in $\frac{2}{3}$ of the squares.

Shade in $\frac{3}{4}$ of the circles.

Shade in $\frac{2}{3}$ of the squares.

Shade in $\frac{3}{4}$ of the circles.

More Tic-Tac-Toe Math

Game 39

Shade in $\frac{3}{4}$ of the squares. □ □ □ □ □ □ □ □ $\frac{3}{4}$ of 8 =	$\frac{3}{4} = \dfrac{\square}{8}$	Shade in $\frac{3}{8}$ of the circles. ○ ○ ○ ○ ○ ○ ○ ○
$\frac{3}{4} + \frac{3}{8} =$	What is I smallest number of crayons I can have if $\frac{2}{8}$ of them are blue, $\frac{1}{4}$ are red, and $\frac{1}{2}$ are orange.	$\frac{3}{4} - \frac{3}{8} =$
$\frac{1}{2} = \dfrac{\square}{8}$	$\frac{3}{4} = \dfrac{\square}{8}$ $\frac{1}{2} = \dfrac{\square}{8}$ $+ \frac{3}{8} = \dfrac{\square}{8}$ —————— $\dfrac{\square}{8} = 1\dfrac{\square}{8}$	$\begin{array}{r}\frac{3}{4}\\[4pt]-\ \frac{1}{2}\\\hline\end{array}$

More Tic-Tac-Toe Math

Game 40

Place a small X to show $\frac{5}{8}$ of an inch.	Place a small circle to show $\frac{7}{16}$ of an inch.	Which is greater? $\frac{5}{8}$ or $\frac{7}{16}$
$\frac{5}{8} - \frac{7}{16} =$	$\frac{7}{16} + \boxed{} = \frac{5}{8}$	If you added $\frac{5}{8}$ of an inch and $\frac{7}{16}$ of an inch, would you have more than 1 inch?
$\frac{5}{8} = \dfrac{\boxed{}}{16}$	Write the answer in lowest terms. $\frac{2}{16} =$	Write the answer in lowest terms. $\frac{10}{16} =$

Game 41

If one dollar is divided equally among five girls, how many cents does each girl get?	$\frac{1}{5}$ of a dollar is _____ cents.	If one dollar is divided equally among four boys, how many cents does each boy get?
$\frac{1}{4}$ of a dollar is _____ cents.	I saved $\frac{3}{5}$ of a dollar each day for a year. How much had I saved at the end of the year?	Which is greater? $\frac{1}{5}$ or $\frac{1}{4}$
$\frac{3}{5}$ of a dollar is _____ cents.	$\frac{3}{4}$ of a dollar is _____ cents.	How many more cents are in $\frac{3}{4}$ of a dollar than in $\frac{3}{5}$ of a dollar?

Game 42

$\dfrac{2}{3} = \dfrac{\boxed{}}{12}$	$\dfrac{3}{4} = \dfrac{\boxed{}}{12}$	$\dfrac{1}{2} = \dfrac{\boxed{}}{12}$
$\begin{aligned} \dfrac{2}{3} &= \dfrac{\boxed{}}{\boxed{}} \\ \dfrac{3}{4} &= \dfrac{\boxed{}}{\boxed{}} \\ + \dfrac{1}{2} &= \dfrac{\boxed{}}{\boxed{}} \\ \hline & \dfrac{\boxed{}}{12} = 1\,\dfrac{\boxed{}}{12} \end{aligned}$	I have 24 marbles. $\frac{1}{4}$ are red. $\frac{1}{3}$ are blue. The rest are yellow. How many yellow marbles do I have?	$\dfrac{3}{4} - \dfrac{2}{3} =$ $\dfrac{\boxed{}}{\boxed{}} - \dfrac{\boxed{}}{\boxed{}} = \dfrac{\boxed{}}{\boxed{}}$
Circle the greatest number. $\dfrac{2}{3} \quad \dfrac{3}{4} \quad \dfrac{1}{2}$	$\dfrac{3}{4}$ of 12 = $\dfrac{2}{3}$ of 12 =	$\dfrac{2}{3} \times \dfrac{3}{4} \times \dfrac{1}{2} =$

Game 43

$\frac{1}{4}$ of 24 =	$\frac{3}{4}$ of 24 =	$\frac{1}{3}$ of 24 =
$\frac{2}{3}$ of 24 =	If September first is on a Monday, what day of the week represents $\frac{5}{6}$ of the month?	$\frac{1}{6}$ of 24 =
$\frac{5}{6}$ of 24 =	$\frac{1}{8}$ of 24 =	$\frac{7}{8}$ of 24 =

Game 44

$\frac{1}{3}$ of 36 =	$\frac{1}{4}$ of 36 =	$\frac{1}{6}$ of 36 =
$\frac{1}{9}$ of 36 =	How much more is $\frac{5}{9}$ of 36 than $\frac{5}{12}$ of 36?	$\frac{2}{3}$ of 36 =
$\frac{3}{4}$ of 36 =	$\frac{5}{6}$ of 36 =	$\frac{7}{9}$ of 36 =

More Tic-Tac-Toe Math

Game 45

If $\frac{1}{5}$ of a number equals 20, what does $\frac{3}{5}$ of that number equal?	If $\frac{3}{5}$ of a number equals 30, what does $\frac{1}{5}$ of the number equal?	If $\frac{1}{5}$ of a number equals 5, what is the number?
What is $\frac{1}{5}$ of 30?	Put 1, 2, 3, or 4 in each box to make the equation true. $$\frac{\square}{\square} + \frac{\square}{\square} = \frac{11}{12}$$	What is $\frac{3}{5}$ of 30?
What is $\frac{4}{5}$ of 30?	What is $\frac{2}{5}$ of 30?	If $\frac{2}{5}$ of a number equals 50, what is the number?

Name _____

Game 46

If $\frac{1}{4}$ of a number equals 10, what does $\frac{3}{4}$ of the number equal?	If $\frac{3}{4}$ of a number equals 75, what does $\frac{1}{4}$ of the number equal?	If $\frac{1}{4}$ of a number equals 5, what is the number?
What is $\frac{1}{4}$ of 28?	Put 1, 2, 4, or 4 in each box to make the equation true. $$\frac{\square}{\square} - \frac{\square}{\square} = \frac{5}{12}$$	What is $\frac{3}{4}$ of 12?
$\frac{1}{4}$ of $\boxed{}$ = 4	What is $\frac{4}{4}$ of 10?	$\frac{3}{4}$ of $\boxed{}$ = 18

Game 47

How much more is $\frac{1}{4}$ of 12 than $\frac{1}{4}$ of 8?	How much less is $\frac{1}{3}$ of 12 than $\frac{1}{3}$ of 21?	Multiply $\frac{3}{4}$ of 20 and $\frac{2}{3}$ of 15.
Multiply $\frac{2}{3}$ of 12 by $\frac{3}{4}$ of 12.	How many cents is $\frac{1}{4}$ of a dollar plus $\frac{1}{5}$ of a quarter minus $\frac{1}{2}$ of a dime?	Add $\frac{5}{6}$ of 30 and $\frac{5}{6}$ of 24.
How much more is $\frac{3}{5}$ of 10 than $\frac{1}{4}$ of 20?	How much less is $\frac{1}{6}$ of 12 than $\frac{1}{3}$ of 12?	Does $\frac{1}{3} + \frac{1}{4} = \frac{2}{7}$?

Name _____

Game 48

What is a fraction?	What is a mixed number?	What is a denominator?
What is a numerator?	Circle the fractions that are *not* written in lowest terms.	What is an improper fraction?
What is a reciprocal?	What is an equivalent fraction?	What is a proper fraction?

Game 49

$\frac{2}{3}$ of 24 means to divide 24 into ___ parts and then multiply by ___.	$\frac{2}{3}$ of 24 =	$\frac{1}{3}$ of 24 means to divide _____ into 3 parts and then multiply by _____.
$\frac{2}{3}$ of a class of 24 students were absent. How many students were absent?	What is the fewest number of candies in a package if $\frac{1}{4}$ are red, $\frac{1}{3}$ are brown, $\frac{1}{6}$ are yellow, $\frac{1}{9}$ are orange, and all the rest are green?	$\frac{1}{3}$ of 24 =
$\frac{2}{3}$ of a class of 24 students were absent. How many students attended class?	$\frac{1}{3}$ of 12 = $\frac{2}{3}$ of 12 =	$\frac{2}{3}$ of 36 = $\frac{1}{3}$ of 36 =

Name _____

Game 50

Circle the fraction that is greater than $\frac{1}{2}$. $\frac{3}{8}$ $\frac{3}{6}$ $\frac{7}{12}$ $\frac{2}{4}$	$\frac{3}{4} = \frac{\square}{12}$	Put these fractions in order from least to greatest. $\frac{1}{2}$ $\frac{3}{8}$ $\frac{1}{4}$ $\frac{1}{8}$ $\frac{3}{4}$
Circle the fractions that equal $\frac{2}{3}$. $\frac{9}{12}$ $\frac{8}{12}$ $\frac{4}{6}$ $\frac{6}{8}$	How many minutes are in $\frac{1}{4}$ of an hour plus $\frac{1}{3}$ of an hour?	Write the answer in lowest terms. $\frac{10}{6} =$
Put these fractions in order from greatest to least. $\frac{5}{12}$ $\frac{1}{3}$ $\frac{1}{2}$ $\frac{3}{4}$ $\frac{5}{6}$	$\frac{5}{6} = \frac{10}{\boxed{}}$	Circle the fractions that equal $\frac{1}{4}$. $\frac{4}{8}$ $\frac{3}{12}$ $\frac{2}{6}$ $\frac{2}{8}$

Measurement

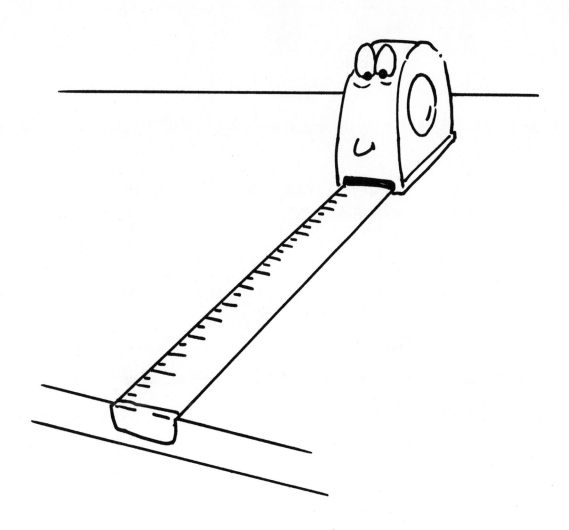

Name _____

Game 51

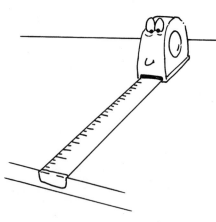

1 pound = _____ ounces.	Which is more? 20 quarts or 6 gallons	64 ounces = _____ pounds
1 gallon = ___ quarts	Estimate in inches the height of your teacher. If your estimate is within 5 inches of the actual height, is it considered correct?	64 quarts = _____ gallons
1 yard = ___ feet	1 mile = _____ feet	36 feet = _____ yards

© Dale Seymour Publications®

More Tic-Tac-Toe Math

Name _____

Game 52

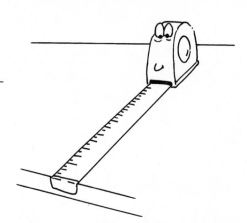

A = _____ inch
B = _____ inch
C = _____ inch
D = _____ inch

The inch on the ruler at the left is divided into _____ parts.

Another name for $\frac{6}{16}$ on a ruler is

$\frac{\square}{\square}$.

Another name for $\frac{1}{4}$ on a ruler is

$\frac{\square}{\square}$.

How many inches are in a mile?

H = _____ inch
I = _____ inch
J = _____ inch

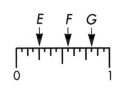

E = _____ inch
F = _____ inch
G = _____ inch

Another name for $\frac{4}{16}$ on a ruler is

$\frac{\square}{4}$.

Another name for $\frac{8}{16}$ on a ruler is

$\frac{\square}{2}$.

© Dale Seymour Publications®

More Tic-Tac-Toe Math

Game 53

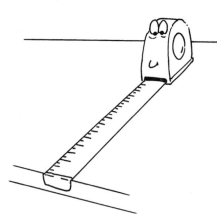

What is the measure of N on this 1-inch ruler? N ↓ 0 1 N= _____ inch	Complete the phrase. 36 i _____ in 1 y _____	The inch ruler on the left is divided into _____ parts. A half inch is divided into _____ parts.
Is the statement true or false? $\frac{3}{4}$ of an inch is longer than $\frac{5}{8}$ of an inch.	A farmer counted his ducks and cows. He saw 26 legs but only 9 heads. How many ducks did he see? How many cows?	Complete the pattern. $\frac{1}{16}$, $\frac{1}{8}$, $\frac{3}{16}$, $\frac{1}{4}$, $\frac{5}{16}$, ___, $\frac{7}{16}$, ___, $\frac{9}{16}$, $\frac{5}{8}$, $\frac{11}{16}$, ___
Another name for two-sixteenths on a ruler is _____ .	Estimate how many inches it is from the floor to the doorknob on the door to your classroom. If your estimate is within 5 inches of the actual measure, is it considered correct?	Another name for four-sixteenths on a ruler is _____ .

Game 54

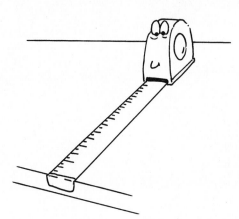

What is the measure of *N* on this 1-inch ruler? *N* ↓ 0 1 *N*= _____ inch	0 1 Use an arrow to show $\frac{7}{8}$ of an inch.	What is the measure of *N* on this 1-inch ruler? *N* ↓ 0 1 *N*= _____ inch
0 1 Use an arrow to show $\frac{5}{16}$ of an inch.	How many comic books does Tia buy if she buys twice as many as Karl? Karl buys 3 fewer than Sam but 3 more than Lily. Sam buys 10 comic books.	What is the measure of *N* on this 2-inch ruler? *N* ↓ 0 1 2 *N*= _____ inch
What is the measure of *N* on this 1-inch ruler? *N* ↓ 0 1 *N*= _____ inch	0 1 Use an arrow to show $\frac{1}{8}$ of an inch.	0 1 2 Use an arrow to show $1\frac{7}{16}$ inches.

More Tic-Tac-Toe Math

Game 55

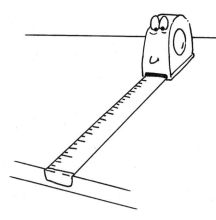

What is the measure of N on this 1-inch ruler?

N

0   1

N= _____ inch

---

0   1

Use an arrow to show $\frac{7}{16}$ of an inch.

What is the measure of N on this 1-inch ruler?

N

0   1

N= _____ inch

---

0   1

Use an arrow to show $\frac{3}{16}$ of an inch.

The average male heart weighs 11 ounces and beats about 70 times per minute. How many times did an average male's heart beat in 1992?

What is the measure of N on this 2-inch ruler?

N

0   1   2

N= _____ inch

What is the measure of N on this 1-inch ruler?

N

0   1

N= _____ inch

---

0   1

Use an arrow to show $\frac{5}{8}$ of an inch.

---

0   1   2

Use an arrow to show $1\frac{1}{8}$ inches.

More Tic-Tac-Toe Math

Name _____

Game 56

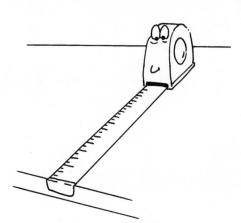

What is the measure of N on this centimeter ruler? N=_____ centimeters	3.7 cm = _____ mm	What is the measure of N on this centimeter ruler? N=_____ millimeters
1 cm = _____ mm	Give the number that each metric prefix represents. kilo _____ hecto _____ deci _____	25 mm = _____ cm
What is the measure of N on this centimeter ruler? N=_____ millimeters	10 mm = ___ cm	What is the measure of N on this centimeter ruler? N=_____ centimeters

More Tic-Tac-Toe Math

Game 57

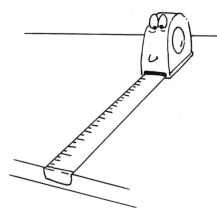

It is 7:30 P.M. How much time will have gone by when it is 4:00 A.M.?	List the months that have 31 days.	It is December 27. In 10 days the date will be _____ .
Write the answer in lowest terms. 7 hours, 14 minutes +8 hours, 52 minutes	A frog jumps 3, then 6, then 12, then 24 centimeters. If it continues in this pattern, how many jumps will it make to travel 1 meter?	Multiply the number of days in a normal year by the number of hours in six days.
If it is 1:15 P.M., what time was it 80 minutes ago?	What is the sum of the years in a century and the years in a decade?	It is October 25. What date was it 40 days ago?

Game 58

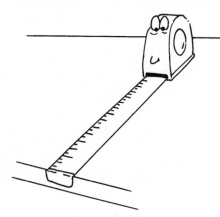

Add the number of days in February, March, and December. Assume it is a leap year.	Write the answer in lowest terms. 20 hours, 38 minutes +22 hours, 39 minutes	How many seconds are in a normal year?
Write the answer in lowest terms. 38 minutes, 20 seconds – 19 minutes, 25 seconds	A frog begins to jump, and each jump is twice the distance of the previous jump. How long is the sixth jump if the first jump was six inches?	If this year is 1998, what year was 2000 years ago?
Abraham Lincoln used these words in a famous speech: "Four score and seven years. . ." How many years is that?	How many minutes are in 575 hours?	If it is 3:00 P.M. in Little Rock, Arkansas, what time is it in Fairfax, Virginia?

Name _____

Game 59

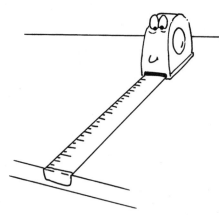

Draw a 120° angle.	Estimate the measure of ∠ABC? C A B	Draw a 30° angle.
An angle that measures between 90° and 180° is called _____ .	List all the leap years since 1950.	An angle that measures between 0° and 90° is called _____ .
Draw a 50° angle.	Estimate the measure of ∠ABC? C A B	Draw a 135° angle.

More Tic-Tac-Toe Math

68

Game 60

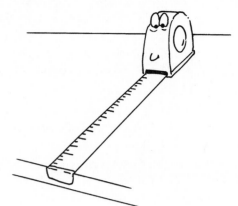

Draw a 45° angle.	What is the measure of ∠ABC?	Draw a 110° angle.
Is ∠ABC acute or obtuse?	Six people enter a tennis tournament. If each person plays every other person only once, how many matches are played?	Is the statement true or false? This angle is called a left angle.
Draw a 150° angle.	What is the measure of ∠ABC?	Draw a 60° angle.

Game 61

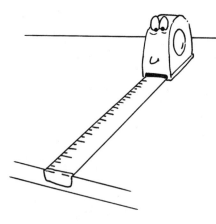

area = _____

perimeter = _____

---

area = _____

perimeter = _____

What does *area* mean?

Draw in the squares to show an area of 9.

perimeter = _____

How many squares does it take to have a perimeter of 10 units?

---

area = _____

perimeter = _____

What does *perimeter* mean?

Add a square so that the perimeter is 14 units and the area is 7 square units.

Draw a picture showing an area of 4 square units, with a perimeter of 8 units.

© Dale Seymour Publications®

Name _____

Game 62

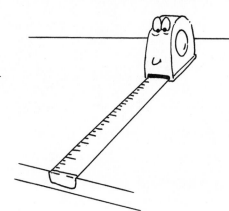

2.5 cm (rectangle, 4.2 cm) area = _____ perimeter = _____	Which is greater, the number of inches in 6 feet or the number of inches in 3 yards?	The area of a rectangle is 12 square centimeters, and the perimeter is 26 centimeters. The length of the rectangle is ____, and the width is ____.
(cube, 1 cm × 1 cm × 1 cm) volume = _____ surface area = ____	Bicycles have 2 wheels, and cars have 4 (not counting the spare). One day I counted 24 wheels as I watched the road. List all the combinations of bicycles and cars I might have seen.	Does 0.26 equal .26?
A farmer had 45 sheep. If all but 10 died, how many were left?	The _____ of a rectangle is the inside region. The _____. of a rectangle is the distance around the outside edges.	Which is longer, 5 centimeters or 4 inches?

More Tic-Tac-Toe Math

Visualization

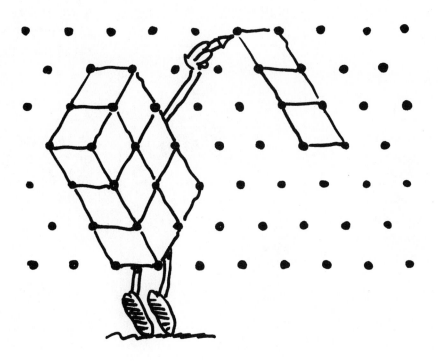

Game 63

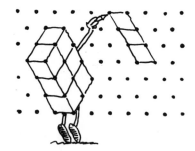

How many squares?

total = ___

☐ = ___

☐ = ___

How many squares?

total = ___

☐ = ___   ☐ = ___

☐ = ___

If this pattern continues, how many small squares will be in the tenth drawing?

Draw in the lines to show the squares inside this rectangle. What is the area?

Show drawing 6.

Draw a rectangle with an area of 10 square units and a perimeter of 14 units.

Draw a square with an area of 16 square units and a perimeter of 16 units.

Draw a square with 16 dots inside.

If this pattern continues, how many dots will be inside the tenth drawing?

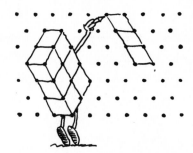

Game 64

Draw a cube. It's edge should be one unit.	Draw two cubes connected to each other. Do two different drawings.	Draw three cubes connected in an L shape.
Draw 4 cubes in a 2-by-2-by-1	Draw 8 cubes in a 2-by-2-by-2 arrangement.	volume = _____ surface area = _____
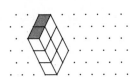 volume = _____ surface area = _____	Draw an arrangement of cubes having a volume of 4 and a surface area of 18.	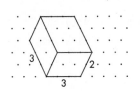 volume = _____ surface area = _____

More Tic-Tac-Toe Math

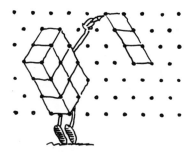

Game 65

Place a dot at (3, 2).	Name the coordinates.	Place a dot at (0, 3).
Name the coordinates.	My car gets 35 miles per gallon of gas. If gas costs $1.27 per gallon, how much will the gas cost me to go 2800 miles?	Name the coordinates.
Place a dot at (6, ⁻2).	Name the coordinates.	Place a dot at (⁻2, 6).

More Tic-Tac-Toe Math

Name _____

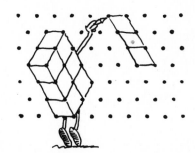

Game 66

Place a dot at (5, 1). 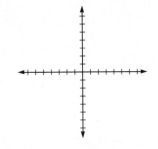	Name the coordinates. 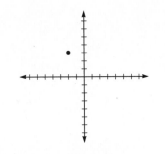	Place a dot at (⁻4, ⁻3). 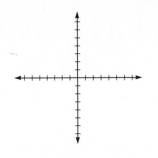
Name the coordinates. 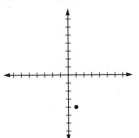	The perimeter of a rectangle is 164 feet. The length is 10 feet more than the width. length = _____ width = _____	Name the coordinates. 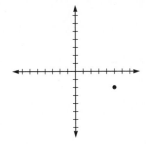
Place a dot at (2, ⁻4). 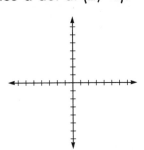	Name the coordinates. 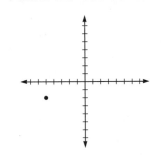	Place a dot at (⁻4, 5). 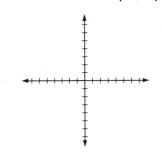

Miscellaneous Problems

Game 67

Sum is to difference as product is to _____ .	V is to 5 as ___ is to 10.	3 is to 9 as ___ is to 16. The answer is *not* 10.
3 is to triangle as 6 is to _____ .	If this pattern continues, how many cubes will there be when the tallest stack has 10 cubes?	= is to *equals* as ___ is to *approximately.*
Product is to multiplication as _____ is to division.	Quarter is to a dollar as quart is to _____ .	Penny is to dime as dime is to _____ .

Name _____

Game 68

If $A > B$ $A + B = 16$ $A \times B = 55$, then $A - B =$	There were 9 rows of seats in a room. There were 6 seats in the first row. Each row after the first one had 7 more seats than the row in front of it. How many seats were in the eighth row?	If $A = 1$ $B = 2$ $C = 3$ and if this pattern continues, what is this word? *6 9 6 20 25*
What do these numbers have in common? 2 3 5 7 11	I bought a TV for $50 more than half of the original price. I paid $300 for the TV. What was the original price?	$ 3. 8 9 x 1 5 ☐ ☐ ☐ ☐ ☐ ☐ ☐ $ ☐ ☐ . ☐ ☐
☐ $\div$ 4 + 6 = 16	Which is greatest? a. 2 gallons b. 12 pints c. 9 quarts	Half of your answer for the top right square multiplied by $\frac{1}{4}$ of your answer for the bottom left square.

Game 69

What is the sum of the days in September, April, June, and November?	I earn 1¢ on Monday, 1¢ on Tuesday, 2¢ on Wednesday, 3¢ on Thursday, 5¢ on Friday, and 8¢ on Saturday. If I work every day and this pattern continues, how much will I have earned by the end of the second week?	Find the average of $1.25, $2.30, $3.35, $4.40, $5.45, and $7.25.
60¢ is what fraction of a dollar? Write the answer in lowest terms.	How many triangles? 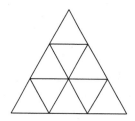	Place a dot at (⁻3, 5). 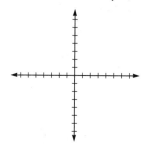
A computer that usually sells for $1296 was on sale for $599.95. Choose the best estimate of the difference between the two prices. $1800, $600, $700, $800	The inside region of this rectangle is the _____ . 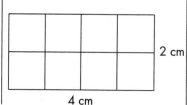 4 cm 2 cm	A car traveled 512 miles in eight hours. What was the average speed for the car?

Game 70

What is the difference between perimeter and area?	3 cm If the perimeter is 16 centimeters, how long is the bottom edge?	If $A \div B = 4$ $A + B = 15$ then $A \times B = $ ◻
About how many millimeters long is this line segment? •————————• a. 4 b. 0.2 c. 40 d. 100	A teacher has 15 packages of construction paper, with 28 pieces in each package. If 30 students share the paper equally, how many sheets of paper will each student receive?	How much less is $\sqrt{64}$ than $6^2 \times 5$?
If I complete pages 5, 6, 7, 8, and 9 of a workbook, how many sheets of paper have I worked on?	Write 360 as the product of prime factors.	Numbers that fit the pattern 1, 4, 9, 25... are called _____ numbers.

Game 71

What is the difference between a prime number and a composite number?	2 cm 3 cm perimeter = _____ area = _____	If $A \times B = 100$ $A + B = 15$ then $A - B = $ ☐ (A is larger than B.)
Circle the least number. 0.7 0.09 0.357 0.105	In a race, 4 out of every 7 runners finish. At that rate, how many finish if there are 42 runners in the race?	How much more is XIX + 5^2 than XVI − 2^3?
A farmer had 57 sheep. All but 8 died. How many lived?	Write 252 as a product of prime factors.	What is the sum of the first 3 square numbers and the first 5 prime numbers?

Game 72

Fill in each box with +, −, x, or ÷. 12 ☐ 12 = 144 12 ☐ 12 = 24	Unscramble this math word. CROUPTD What does it mean?	1 → 1 4 → 8 9 → 27 16 → 64 What comes next in this pattern? ☐ → ☐
The number of vertices on a cube + the number of sides on a decagon. = _____	Complete the phrase. 24 h _____ in a d _____	$12 \times$ ☐ $= 84$ $84 \div 12 =$ ☐ $84 \div 7 =$ ☐
I am a triangular number and also a multiple of 11. I have exactly four factors. What number am I?	3 is to 5 as 24 is to _____ . The answer is *not* 26.	How much more is $(5 + 4)^2$ than $5^2 + 4^2$?

Game 73

Find the average of the first seven square numbers.

I earned 1¢ on Monday, 4¢ on Tuesday, 9¢ on Wednesday, 16¢ on Thursday, and 25¢ on Friday. If this pattern continues, how much will I earn on Sunday?

If $A = 4$
$B = 3$
$C = 2$
$D = 1$
Find the average of these grades: C, C, B, A, D, C, C, C, A, A, B, D, C, A, C, C, A, A, B, and A. What letter grade is that?

0.75 is the decimal name for what fraction?

How many small cubes are in this block?

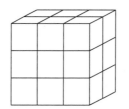

Name the coordinates.

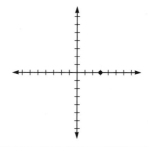

I mailed five packages. Each package weighed between 8 pounds and 12 pounds. What is a reasonable estimate of the total weight of the 5 packages?

a. less than 20 pounds
b. more than 60 pounds
c. between 40 and 60 pounds
d. between 20 and 40 pounds

In the drawing above, the math word for the number of small cubes that are in the block is

_____ .

I get a special rate of $19.75 for 9 tickets. What is the approximate cost per ticket at this rate?

a. $3.50
b. $2.00
c. $4.00
d. $5.00

More Tic-Tac-Toe Math

Game 74

Define *equivalent*.	Which pairs of fractions are equivalent? $\frac{1}{2}$ $\frac{1}{2}$ $\frac{1}{3}$ $\frac{2}{6}$ $\frac{2}{4}$ $\frac{2}{5}$	What number does N represent? N $\downarrow$ 0 1 2

Write the answer in lowest terms.
 	
   3 gallons, 2 quarts
+ 1 gallon, 3 quarts
_____
	If $A = 4B$
	
	     $B = 6C$
	
	then
	
	$A + B = \boxed{} C$
	
	(Use smallest whole number possible.)
		A cube has ___ faces and ___ corners.

Circle the least fraction. $\frac{1}{3}$ $\frac{1}{4}$ $\frac{1}{2}$ $\frac{1}{5}$	[rectangle] 1.4 cm 3.2 cm perimeter = _____ area = _____	$20\% =$ a. $\frac{1}{4}$ b. $\frac{1}{2}$ c. $\frac{1}{5}$ d. $\frac{3}{5}$

Game 75

Complete the phrase. 16 o _____ in a p _____	Unscramble this word: TAMOSITIEN	7 → 42. 12 → 72. ☐ → 24
Is the statement true or false? There are 8 pints in a gallon.	If I earn 1¢ on day one, 2¢ on day two, 4¢ on day three, 8¢ on day four, on what day will I earn $10.24?	If my car goes 32 miles and uses only one gallon of gas, how far can it go on 15 gallons of gas?
9 x ☐ = 108 108 ÷ 9 = ☐ 108 ÷ 12 = ☐	Which number does not belong? 2 3 5 7 8	Penney is to dollar as centimeter is to _____.

Game 76

I am a two-digit number. I am a multiple of 10, and I have exactly 8 factors. I am divisible by 3. What number am I ?	Is the statement true or false? Exactly 7 months of the year have 31 days.	List the six factors of 12. Multiply them. What is the product?
Do not use a calculator. 0.285 + 0.49 + 2.04 + 20.5 =	I am thinking of a number. It has two digits. When I reverse the digits and then add the new number to the original number, I get 44. What is the number?	Is the statement true or false? The decimal name for $\frac{1}{2}$ is 0.05.
What is the sum of all the multiples of 6 between 20 and 40?	Is the statement true or false? 0.05 is between 0.5 and 0.6.	How many numbers lower than 100 either begin or end with five?

Game 77

If ☐ + △ = 9

☐ – △ = 4,

then

☐ = ___ and

△ = ___ .

Which letter represents 0.75?

0   1

    A   B   C

Which number does not belong?

11
13
15
17
19

What is the least number that is divisible by 2, 3, 4, and 5?

Complete the phrase.

90 d _____

in a r _____ a_____

I have $2.25 in dimes and quarters. I have two more quarters than dimes. How many quarters and dimes do I have?

Which is least?

$\sqrt{81}$
XIV
3^2
2^3
10

What do these numbers have in common?

16
4
64
100
49

$$\begin{array}{r} 3\ \square\ 1\ \square \\ -\ \ \ 8\ 7\ 5 \\ \hline 2\ 1\ \square\ 9 \end{array}$$

Game 78

 1 2 3 If this pattern continues how many circles will be in the tenth drawing?	☐ x 7 + 5 = 54	If A = 1 B = 2 C = 3 and if this pattern continues, what is this math word? <u>19</u> <u>17</u> <u>21</u> <u>1</u> <u>18</u> <u>5</u>
What do these numbers have in common? 45 27 81 126	Cookies sell one for $1 or ten for $8. What is the lowest price I could pay for 28 cookies?	The thermometer reads 40 degrees above zero. If the weather gets colder and the temperature drops 56 degrees, what does the thermometer read?
A tray holds 12 salads. How many trays are needed to hold salads for 250 people?	☐ − 28 ☐ x 2 60	5) 9 0 0 5

© Dale Seymour Publications®

Game 79

Fill in each box with +, −, x, or ÷.

8 ☐ 7 =15

8 ☐ 7 = 56

Unscramble this math word:

BTOSTURCANI

---

96 → 12

32 → 4

20 → 2.5

What rule explains this?

The number of feet in a mile times the number of inches in a yard equals

☐

Complete the phrase.

12 m _____

in a y _____

---

8 x ☐ = 56

56 ÷ 8 = ☐

56 ÷ 7 = ☐

I am a square number. I have exactly 9 factors. I am greater than 5^2 but less than 5 x 10. What number am I?

---

2 is to 3 as 12 is to _____ .

The answer is *not* 13.

How much less is 16 − 2 x 5

than

(35 + 56) ÷ 7?

More Tic-Tac-Toe Math

Game 80

What is the freezing point of water on a Fahrenheit thermometer?	How many zeroes are in the number for a googol?	What is the boiling point for water on a Fahrenheit thermometer?
What math word means "going on forever" or "having no end"?	If it takes five minutes to cut a log into four pieces, how long will it take to cut the log into 10 pieces?	How far does light travel in one second?
What is the boiling point for water on a Celsius thermometer?	What is the Spanish word for *two*?	What is the freezing point for water on the Celsius thermometer?

Game 81

☐ little pigs + ☐ dwarfs = ☐	How many acres are in a *section* of land?	☐ inches in a yard x ☐ quarters in a dollar =
The number of balls in a pool game times the number of digits in one billion equals _____.	The number of sheets of paper in a ream times the number of sheets of paper in a quire equals _____.	The number of nights in a fortnight times the number of eggs in a gross equals _____.
☐ ounces in 5 pounds – ☐ hours in 3 days =	How many yards are in a *rod?*	The number of legs on 2 centipedes plus the number of legs on an octopus equals _____.

More Tic-Tac-Toe Math

Name _____

Game 82

Cinco is the Spanish word for what number?	Give the answer in English. siete + ocho =	What is the Spanish word for *one*?
Give the answer in English. ocho ÷ cuatro	Give the answer in Spanish. $3^2 =$	Give the answer in English. uno x cuatro
Tres is the Spanish word for what number?	Give the answer in English. nueve – seis =	What is the Spanish word for *ten*?

More Tic-Tac-Toe Math

Game 83

The German word *eins* represents what number?	What is the sum of fünf, sechs, and drei? Write the answer as a number.	Write the answer as a number. sieben – drei =
How much less is eins then vier? Write the number.	How much more is zehn x acht than sechs ÷ eins? Write the answer as a number.	How much more is neun than drei? Write the answer as a number.
What number comes next? Write the German word. zwei, vier, sechs, acht	What is the German word for *ten*?	If you multiply fünf by zwei, what number do you get?

Game 84

Cinq is the French word for what number?	Give the answer in English. trois + deux =	What is the French word for *one*?
Give the answer in English. neuf − sept =	What number comes next? Write the answer as a number. un, deux, quatre, huit	Give the answer in English. dix ÷ cinq =
Dix is the French word for what number?	Give the answer in English. quatre x deux =	What is the French name for *ten*?

Game 85

What word is used for the answer to a multiplication problem?	What is the top part of a fraction?	What is the answer to a division problem?
Unscramble this math word. TALEQUENIVU	If I was born in June of 1944 and this is May of 1994, what is my age in years?	Unscramble this math word. QAEUL
What is the answer to a subtraction problem?	What is the bottom part of a fraction?	What is the answer to an addition problem?

Answer Key

Game 1

24; 108; 12; 3	6 7 or 7 6	25
18; 24	5	600 400 900 1900
24	5,490,000	60

Game 3

8 9 9	63	6 7 8
one hundred million, one thousand, twenty five	13 $2n + 1$ or multiply by 2 and then add 1.	100
1 1 0 8 9	8,182,000	3 6 4 8 4 2 5 6 4 6 2 0 8

Game 2

2 3 5 1 6 9 2 1 4	4	3 0 1 4 1 2 5 6
12	119	4; September, June, April, November
3 2 1 6 8 1 7 92	six billion, five million, four thousand, one.	6)12 0 6

Game 4

600	36	360,540
6	1 + 3 + 5 + 7 + 9 + 11 + 13 + 15 + 17 + 19	17
d. 6^3	5000	178

More Tic-Tac-Toe Math

Game 5

3	$\boxed{6} \times \boxed{8}$ or $\boxed{8} \times \boxed{6}$	128
28; 35	60	$\begin{array}{r} 700 \\ \times\ 60 \\ \hline 42{,}000 \end{array}$
yes	8,700,000	$\begin{array}{r} 585 \\ 7\overline{)4095} \\ \underline{35}\ \ \\ 59\ \\ \underline{56}\ \\ 35 \\ \underline{35} \end{array}$

Game 7

2	1024	18
4	$1 + 2 + 3 + 4$ $+ 5 + 6 + 7$ $+ 8 + 9 + 10$	64
72	b. 8 inches	2190

Game 6

x; +	ADDITION	Multiply by 3.
13 + 50 = 63	16	48 8 6
81	32	45

Game 8

110	Examples: both odd; both are prime; both are between 10 and 20.	3136
$\frac{1}{2}$ a candy bar	5 and 7	2 candy bars
b. 2 ÷ 4	The answer to 4 ÷ 2 is a whole number. The answer to 2 ÷ 4 is a fraction.	a. 4 ÷ 2

Game 9

1; 4; 9; 16; square	2; 6; 24; 120; 720	37
DIVISION	10; 7	12 or 21; (or 30)
1; 4; 9; 16; 25	5; 9; 24; 50; 1000	9; 16; 64; 81

Game 11

1, 2, 4, 5, 8, 10, 16, 20. 40. 80	40, 80, 120, 160, 200	1, 2, 3, 4, 6, 8, 12, 16, 24, 48
80, 160, 240, 320, 400	55	120
60, 120, 180, 240, 300	240	35

Game 10

$3 \times (8 + 6) \div 2 = 21$	Weeks; Month	b. 79
false	$9 \div 3 + 8$	45
0	MATHEMATICS	$10 \times (3 + 2) - 8 = 42$

Game 12

$2^2 \times 3$	d. 32	$2^3 \times 3$
b. 323	7	d. 8
29	c. 32,120	d. 97

Game 13

17	23	$3 \times 3 = 9$
$5 \times 5 \times 5$	January 10	2
2	36	1

Game 15

385	36	because $15 \times 15 = 225$
31	27	13
15	21	$15 = 1 + 2 + 3 + 4 + 5$

Game 14

4280	1000	3000
3100	Fedor is 18, and Mary is 36.	10,000
7.342×10^3	5	scientific notation

Game 16

7 and 8	[3][4] or [4][3]	6 and 7
[5][6] or [6][5]	1	15
3 and 6	6	19, 20, and 21

Game 17

3 underlined; 5 circled	2.13	one hundred three and one thousandth
0.51	70	1.0
1001.05	2.528	0.015, 1.05, 1.5

Game 19

1 underlined; 7 circled	0.56	two thousand, fifteen and twenty-five ten-thousands
5684.00	34 minutes	1.000
505.0500	0.06084	0.25, 2.015, 2.06, 2.5

Game 18

8 underlined; 4 circled	7.879735	three thousand, fifteen and five hundredths
305.5	6	1.00
2002.002	$\begin{array}{r} 0.0038 \\ \times \quad 4.6 \\ \hline 00228 \\ 00152 \\ \hline 0.01748 \end{array}$	30.4, 3.2, 3.14, 3.014

Game 20

The answer should be 0.06	quarts; gallon	the answer should be 20.96.
64; 27; 8; 1	won 14 and lost 6	$8 \rightarrow 4$ $4 \rightarrow 2$ $2 \rightarrow 1$
c. 0.2 + 0.8	FACTOR	yes

Game 21

0.99	$1.94	1.75
8.2	2	11.84
2.8; 3.5	$0.06	$2.39

Game 23

$3.65	$1.60	$0.40
45	30	$4.16
true	$27.30	CALCULATOR

Game 22

0.9	$3.24	1.58
4100	81	8
4.0; 4.8	$0.70	$13.61

Game 24

$3.92	20 for $4.65	103.5
12-ounce cola for $1.20	One possibility: 2 jumbo burgers; 1 medium fries, 1 cola	120
63 or 64 (63.16)	28	$161.50

Game 25

$0.30	$1.90	$22.40
$4.88	12	$4.14
8	0.07	240

Game 27

0.03	143	$11.43
$254.00	30	8
$0.90	$3.75	$2.51

Game 26

$100	$3.60	$.80
$7.71	50	$1.05
100	$18.30	$757.50

Game 28

five thousand, two and sixty-four thousandths	$27.00	<
4.34	$2.70	About $5.00
770 616 6.930	(1 x 10) + (2 x 1) + (3 x .1) + (4 x .01)	20

Game 29

four hundred sixty-nine ten-thousands	$567.12	5.006
3.805	256.0	$21.00
$(7 \times 10^3) + (4 \times 10^2) + (1 \times 10) + (3 \times 1)$	0090 0135 <u>0. 01440</u>	28.4

Game 31

0.342	1.5	50.302
84.537	27 hundredths	1.12
0.95	6	0.015

Game 30

0.12	0.7	2.45
0.0009	0.001	1.5625
$13.14	$\frac{1}{20}$	$46.20

Game 32

4	$\frac{4}{12}$ or $\frac{1}{3}$	0.4
1;1	$2\frac{1}{3}$ cm	2
0.4	$\frac{1}{3}$	4

Game 33

0.5	7	5
25.73	1.65	0.25
2.003	7	63.51

Game 35

x 0.01; 0.01	days; Febuary	0.0525
true	$56.50	10%; $\frac{15}{100}$
$15.00	$101.33	40

Game 34

0.53	yes	4.288
0.06	0.55	0.53
4.288	two tenths	0.06

Game 36

c. 80% of 40 = 30	20%	88%
40	10	$196.00
$2.75	$12.72	b. 5 is 10 % of 50

Game 37

6 circles shaded	4 circles shaded	$\frac{1}{2}$
10	$\frac{2}{12}$ or $\frac{1}{6}$	$\frac{1}{2}$
6	4	$\frac{1}{3}$

Game 39

6 squares shaded; 6	6	3 circles shaded
$\frac{9}{8}$ or $1\frac{1}{8}$	4	$\frac{3}{8}$
4	$\begin{array}{c} \frac{6}{8} \\ \frac{4}{8} \\ \frac{3}{8} \\ \frac{13}{8} = 1\frac{5}{8} \end{array}$	$\frac{2}{8}$ or $\frac{1}{4}$

Game 38

3 circles shaded	10 squares shaded	6 circles shaded
2 squares shaded	15	6 squares shaded
9 circles shaded	4 squares shaded	12 circles shaded

Game 40

ruler 0—1 with x	ruler 0—1 with x	$\frac{5}{8}$
$\frac{3}{16}$	$\frac{3}{16}$	yes
10	$\frac{1}{8}$	$\frac{5}{8}$

More Tic-Tac-Toe Math

Game 41

20	20	25
25	$219 = $219.60 if leap year	$\frac{1}{4}$
60	75	15

Game 43

6	18	8
16	Thursday, September 25	4
20	3	21

Game 42

8	9	6
$\begin{array}{l}\frac{8}{12}\\\frac{9}{12}\\\frac{6}{12}\\\hline\frac{23}{12}=1\frac{11}{12}\end{array}$	10	$\frac{9}{12}-\frac{8}{12}=\frac{1}{12}$
$\frac{3}{4}$	9; 8	$\frac{1}{4}$

Game 44

12	9	6
4	5	24
27	30	28

Game 45

60	10	25
6	$\frac{1}{4} + \frac{2}{3}$	18
24	12	125

Game 47

1	3	150
72	$0.25	45
1	2	no

Game 46

30	25	20
7	$\frac{2}{3} - \frac{1}{4}$	9
16	10	24

Game 48

part of a whole	a whole number and a fraction	bottom part of a fraction
top part of a fraction	$\frac{6}{8}, \frac{4}{6}, \frac{8}{12}, \frac{6}{9}, \frac{10}{6}, \frac{2}{1}$	a fraction in which the numerator is greater than the denominator
a fraction that has been flipped over	a fraction that has the same value as another but uses different numbers	a fraction in which the numerator is less than the denominator

Game 49

3; 2	16	24; 1
16	36	8
8	4; 8	24; 12

Game 51

16	6 gallons	4
4	Answers will vary.	16
3	5280	12

Game 50

$\frac{7}{12}$	9	$\frac{1}{8}$, $\frac{1}{4}$, $\frac{3}{8}$, $\frac{1}{2}$, $\frac{3}{4}$
$\frac{8}{12}$, $\frac{4}{6}$	35	$1\frac{2}{3}$
$\frac{5}{6}$, $\frac{3}{4}$, $\frac{1}{2}$, $\frac{5}{12}$, $\frac{1}{3}$	12	$\frac{3}{12}$, $\frac{2}{8}$

Game 52

$\frac{1}{8}$; $\frac{1}{2}$; $\frac{11}{16}$; $\frac{7}{8}$	16	$\frac{3}{8}$
$\frac{2}{8}$ or $\frac{4}{16}$	63,360	$\frac{3}{16}$; $\frac{3}{8}$; $\frac{3}{4}$
$\frac{1}{4}$; $\frac{9}{16}$; $\frac{13}{16}$	$\frac{1}{4}$	$\frac{1}{2}$

Game 53

$\frac{3}{8}$	inches; yard	16; 8
true	5: 4	$\frac{3}{8}$; $\frac{1}{2}$; $\frac{3}{4}$
one-eighth or $\frac{1}{8}$	Answers will vary.	$\frac{1}{4}$ or $\frac{2}{8}$

Game 55

$\frac{1}{16}$	[ruler diagram]	$\frac{15}{16}$
[ruler diagram]	36,892,800 (1992 was a leap year.)	$1\frac{3}{8}$
1	[ruler diagram]	[ruler diagram]

Game 54

$\frac{1}{2}$	[ruler diagram]	$\frac{5}{8}$
[ruler diagram]	14	$1\frac{1}{4}$
$\frac{3}{4}$	[ruler diagram]	[ruler diagram]

Game 56

2.5	37	13
10	1000; 100; 0.1 or $\frac{1}{10}$	2.5
32	1	1.8

Game 57

$8\frac{1}{2}$	January, March, May, July, August, October, December	January 6
16 hours, 6 minutes	16	52, 560
11:55 A.M.	110	September 16

Game 59

	20°	
obtuse	Every four years starting with 1952	acute
	100°	

Game 58

91	43 hours, 17 minutes	31,536,000
18 minutes, 55 seconds	192 inches	1 B.C.
87	34,500	4:00 P.M.

Game 60

	≈ 120°	
obtuse	15 matches	false (no such angle)
	≈ 60°	

Game 61

4 square units; 10 units	3 square units; 12 units	the region inside a polygon
 20	4	4 square units; 10 units
distance around the outside edge of a polygon	 Example	

Game 63

5 4 1	13 9 4 1	100
 A = 18		2 .5.
4 4		100

Game 62

10.5 cm²; 13.4 cm	the number of inches in 3 yards	12 centimeters; of 1 centimeter; 1 centimeter or 12 centimeters
1 cm³; 6 cm²	Bikes | Cars 12 | 0 10 | 1 8 | 2 6 | 3 4 | 4 2 | 5 0 | 6	yes
10	area; perimeter	4 inches

Game 64

Examples 	Examples 	Examples
Example 	Example 	6 cubes; 26 squares
6 cubes 22 squares	Examples 	18 cubes 42 squares

Game 65

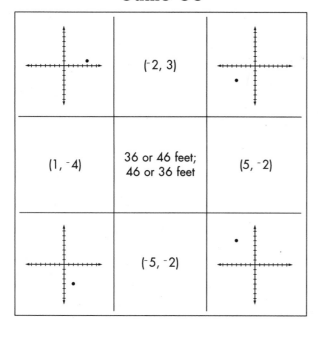	(2, 3)	✛
(⁻2, 3)	$101.60	(⁻4, 1)
✛	(⁻2, ⁻4)	✛

Game 67

quotient	X	4
hexagon	55	≈
quotient	gallon	dollar

Game 66

✛	(⁻2, 3)	✛
(1, ⁻4)	36 or 46 feet; 46 or 36 feet	(5, ⁻2)
✛	(⁻5, ⁻2)	✛

Game 68

6	55	FIFTY
They are prime.	$500	1945 389 $58.35
40	c. 9 quarts	250

More Tic-Tac-Toe Math

116

Game 69

120	$9.86	$4.00
$\frac{3}{5}$	13	
$700	area	64 miles per hour

Game 71

A prime number has exactly two factors. A composite number has more than two factors	6 cm²;10 cm	21
0.09	24	36
8	2 x 2 x 3 x 3 x 7 (in any order)	42

Game 70

Perimeter is the distance around a polygon. Area is the inside region.	5 centimeters	36
40	14	172
3	2 x 2 x 2 x 3 x 3 x 5 (in any order)	square

Game 72

x; +	Product; answer to a multiplication problem	25 → 125
18	hours; day	7; 7; 12
55	40	40

Game 73

20	49¢	2.75; either B – or C
$\frac{3}{4}$	18	(3, 0)
c. between 40 and 60 pounds	volume	b. $2.00

Game 75

ounces; pound	ESTIMATION	4
true	day 11	480 miles
12; 12; 9	8 (Others are prime.)	foot

Game 74

equal value	$\frac{1}{3}$ $\frac{2}{6}$	$\frac{3}{4}$ or 0.75
5 gallons, 1 quart	30	6; 8
$\frac{1}{5}$	4.48 cm²; 9.2 cm	c. $\frac{1}{5}$

Game 76

30	true	1728
23.315	13 or 31	false (The decimal for $\frac{1}{2}$ is 0.5.)
90	false (0.55 is between 0.5 and 0.6.)	19

Game 77

6.5; 2.5	C	15 (Others are prime.)
60	degrees; right angle	7 quarters and 5 dimes
2^3	are square numbers	3 0 1 4 − 8 7 5 2 1 3 9

Game 79

+; x	SUBTRACTION	Divide by 8.
190,080	months; year	7; 7; 8
36	18	7

Game 78

55	7	SQUARE
are multiples of 9	$24	−16 degrees or 16 degrees below zero
21	58 − 28 30	1801 5)9005 5 40 40 05 5 0

Game 80

32°	100	212°
infinite	15 minutes	186,000 feet
100°	dos	0°

Game 81

3; 7; 10	640	36 x 4 = 144
15 x 10 = 150	ream = 480 to 516 quire = 24 or 25	14 x 144 = 2016
80 – 72 = 8	5.5	208

Game 83

1	14	4
3	74	6
zehn	zehn	10

Game 82

5	fifteen	uno
two	nueve	four
3	three	diez

Game 84

5	five	un
two	16	two
10	eight	dix

Game 85

product	numerator	quotient
EQUIVALENT	49	EQUAL
difference	denominator	sum